T0208316

Time To Get Up

A collection of poems
to help your kids get out of bed

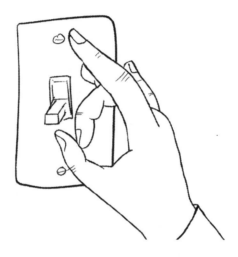

Written by Sterling Porter

Illustrated by Ksenia Porter

authorHOUSE®

AuthorHouse™
1663 Liberty Drive
Bloomington, IN 47403
www.authorhouse.com
Phone: 833-262-8899

Published by AuthorHouse 09/13/2023

ISBN: 979-8-8230-0894-5 (sc)
ISBN: 979-8-8230-0892-1 (hc)
ISBN: 979-8-8230-0893-8 (e)

Library of Congress Control Number: 2023909563

Print information available on the last page.

This book is printed on acid-free paper.

For Parley, Charlotte, Ksenia, Hyrum, Estella, and Ruby

Foreword

My husband is super nerdy, and I apologize in advance.
—Suzanne Porter

Author's note: when I asked my wife to write the foreword to the book, she said, "why don't you just write it, and I'll sign it." She ended up writing it herself.

Introduction

This book was born of adversity. Suzanne and I have six kids, and getting them out of bed is—if not the hardest part of the day—definitely the first part of the day. Like other family activities that are not inherently fun (like chores), it always helps to inject some excitement into the routine. I don't remember the exact poem I came up with first, but I do remember the satisfying groans from my kids which told me I was onto something. Being the "nice" dad and softly coaxing your kids out of bed doesn't work. You have to get their hearts pumping and their brain gears a-turning. Over the years, I've found that painfully annoying poetry is the answer.

This book contains 100 or so "dad" poems along with suggestions for how to deliver them to your kids. The trick is to bring the energy, fully committing to the performance. If you do, your kids will feel how much you love them and how much you wish your stand-up career could have paid the bills. Try these poems out, and I guarantee your creative juices will start flowing. Before you know it, you'll be coming up with your own morning poetry that your kids will regret for the rest of their lives.

How to Use This Book

Keep this book on the nightstand. When you wake up in the morning, open the book to a random page. Read the poem. Imagine yourself reciting the poem. Read the supplemental comments and performance suggestions. If applicable, gather any related props. Reread the poem a few more times, committing it to memory, as a memorized delivery is much more effective than reading it from a page. After you feel comfortable with your approach, head down the hall to your child's bedroom and deliver the performance of a lifetime!

P.S. Don't be discouraged if the poem fails to get your child out of bed. It's not the poem. It's your delivery. Keep working at it!

It's time to get up.
That's a good lad.
Hey, I need your opinion.
Is my morning breath bad?

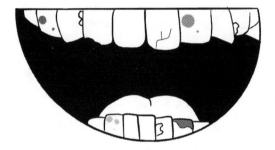

Might want to brush your teeth first, or maybe deliver the poem while brushing your teeth so that you have an excuse to breathe heavily into your child's face if they don't respond right away.

It's time to get up.
It's time to shave my beard.
But I kinda like it scratchy.
Do you think that's weird?

Without delay, lean in close so that your 5 a.m. shadow is right next to your child's cherub cheek. Then give it a brisk rub, and you'll get an honest answer to your question.

It's time to get up!
It's not time to be naughty.
So put a smile on your face,
And go use the potty!

Bathroom humor is a concept that children naturally appreciate. As they grow older, they begin to be influenced by civilizing forces (mother) and lose their innocence. Take advantage of this special time while you can.

It's *not* time to get up.
It's time to sleep.
And to help you out,
Let's count some sheep. Baaaaaa!

It's up to you to assess your kid's tolerance for animal sounds early in the morning. Fortunately, the "baa" sound lends itself to a wide range of dynamics. I suggest standing fairly close to the child's ear and softly baa-ing a few times. The timber should be akin to a cat purring. If the child doesn't rouse, increase both intensity and pitch; you should sound like a sheep-version of your child when he or she is complaining. If necessary, ramp up the volume and frequency to simulate a sheep struggling desperately to escape a pack of wolves.

It's time to get up.
It's not time to snuggle.
Hey, look at these shoes
I'm trying to juggle!

All juggling skill levels are acceptable. I like using girls' strappy sandals
as they provide more to grab as they spin in the air.

It's time to get up!
It's not time to snooze.
Let's play rock, paper, scissors.
You are sure to lose!

My kids love rock, paper, scissors, and I've spent years purposely losing to them to make them believe they have a special talent for the game. Suggesting a rematch in the early morning can awaken their thirst for blood and help them pop out of bed.

It's time to get up!

(pretend to answer your cell phone)

Oh, Hi!
Nah, it's not too early—just gettin' the kids up
Ok...Talk to you later...Bye!

This one will pique your kids' curiosity about who in the world would be calling dear old dad at such an early hour.

It's time to get up!
Don't wanna leave you hangin',
So I'll finish my poem this morning by sayin'…

(promptly leave the room)

There's nothing quite like a cliffhanger to...

It's time to get up!
It's time to get sick!
And to help you out,
Let's give that elbow a lick.

You don't actually have to deliver on this one. Just the threat is enough. However, your kids will love it if you simulate the lick with something wet. Experiment with different textures (e.g. rag, sponge, stick of butter).

It's time to get up!
It's not time to slumber!
Please hold your applause
Until after this number.

(Belt out "O What a Beautiful Morning", or something similar)

My dad inspired this one. A few times a week, my brothers and I would be awakened by a bright light and a fortissimo rendition of the Broadway classic, "O What a Beautiful Morning!"

It's time to get up!
It's not time to cry.
Cheer up, sad face!
I've got a chocolate pie!
I'm sorry—that was a lie.
Now you're going to die.
That was another lie.
No, no, it's ok to cry.
Let me help those tears dry.
Here's my tie.
Dab your eye.
Don't be shy.
Oh my!
Did somebody change the password to the Wi-Fi?!
Now I'm gonna cry!
Ok, bye.

(pause to simulate your absence)

Hi.
It's me, dad guy.
False alarm on the Wi-Fi, by the way.

(deftly slip into an Australian accent)

Wanna know why?
Airplane mode, okay? (uh-kye)

Long-form dad poems are the best, but they don't pop into our heads as readily as the four-liners. Every now and then, though, you latch onto a syllable, like in "cry" or "pie", and the rhyming juices won't stop gushing.

It's time to get up!
It's top o' the mornin'!
I hope these poems
Aren't too painfully bornin'

Before going on stage, take a few moments to rev up your rolly R's and slip into your best Irish accent. Helpful hint: push your voice a bit higher than usual to channel your inner leprechaun.

It's time to get up!
That's a good lass.
To awaken your senses,
Here's some freshly cut grass.

Save a handful of grass from your latest lawn mow. Then get into character by pretending you're a supervillain. Slowly approach your nemesis secret agent who is just coming around after receiving a prior blow to the head. When you apply your special green smelling salts, your captive will snap awake, at which point you can laugh maniacally and launch into a monologue about how ironic it is that even though you're destined to battle each other forever, the struggle, in a way, completes you and that the cosmic forces that brought you together have truly given your life meaning. And before you know it, your little archenemy has given you the slip. You won't get away that easy! I know where you sleep!

It's time to get up!
Doesn't seem like you care.
But you'll change your mind
When I'm a grizzly bear!

I read in an outdoor magazine once that if you stand on your two hind legs and make yourself as big as possible and then make a lot of noise, you'll have a greater chance of waking up your kids.

"Is it time to get up?"
You may ask. "Or is it not?"
You wanna see how full
I filled my tissue with snot?

Best to keep your material relevant, so try to incorporate major life
events like you having a man-cold.

It's time to get up!
It's not time to be sleepy.
So I'll just stand real close
And smile real creepy.

Kids love attention of any kind, so even a good creepy stare will make them feel loved and want to obey your request to get out of bed. Creepiness takes many forms, so I suggest you err on the side of weird-second-cousin creepy as opposed to clown-in-the-sewer creepy.

It's time to get up!
You know, I've been thinking.
Ever wondered how an eyelash feels
When somebody's blinking?

(get real close and blink your lashes on their cheek)

Extra credit if you launch into "Butterfly Kisses" by Bob Carlisle.

It's time to get up!
Come on little Jimmy.
Now pay attention.
Gonna teach you how to shimmy!

Of all the practical knowledge a father can pass down to his children, the dance moves he perfected in junior high rank near the top. For this poem, be sure to choose an especially energetic move, bearing in mind that you're not the limber 14-year-old you used to be.

It's time to get up!
Ever heard of the space shuttle?
No? That's OK—hey!
Scoot over, let's cuddle.

Not every poem needs to be followed by an irritant. Sometimes kids need to snuggle with their dad, OK? And while you're at it, tell them about the space shuttle, its glorious 30-year ride, and the economic forces that led to NASA retiring the program.

It's time to get up!
It's not time to coddle.
And to show you I'm serious,
I've got a spray bottle!

Ah, the spray bottle. So often threatened, so rarely employed. Here's your excuse. It's called poetic license.

It's time to get up!
It's not time to slack.
It looks like you need
Me to scratch your back.

Be careful with this one, as soft scratching can lull a child back to sleep. Best to start off light and end up with a supersonic rub. Nine times out of ten, kids can't help but start humming to themselves just to hear their own voice vibrating.

It's time to get up!
It's not time to lie back.
Look how deftly
I can make my knuckles crack!

Crack away! And don't worry—about half of the studies out there prove that cracking your knuckles won't cause arthritis. The other half you can ignore because they don't fit my world view.

Hey! It's time to get up!
As they say in mother Russia,
If you do not get up,
I will have to crush ya!
(followed by the exclamation Body Slam! and a gentle, actual body slam)

My kids' favorite. Russian accent required.

It's time to get up!
It's not time to bawl.
Let me cheer you up
With my eagle call!

Kuh-KA! (loudly)

You'll want to approximate a Daniel Larusso stance. You're going for maximum volume on this one.

It's time to get up!
It's not time for bed.
Let's head to the kitchen
And eat celery instead.

Waltz into your child's room with a stalk of celery in hand. Keeping cadence with the poem, take a loud crunchy bite. Make sure you bite clean through, as celery has those fibrous strands along the exterior that like to hold on for dear life! If the child does not stir, try explaining this very fascinating feature. Then tie it into a lesson about flossing.

It's time to get up!
It's Christmas day!
New rule this year.
Every gift, a tax you'll pay!

They say "he who has his family near is richest of all", so you should use a tax rate well north of 45%. It's only fair.

It's time to get up!
It's time to look your best.
And that's impossible, my dear,
If you don't get dressed.

A sophisticated English accent works nicely here. In fact, whenever you use an English accent, it never hurts to follow it up with an energetic "Gov'nuh!" or "Brilliant!"

It's time to get up!
Ever seen an armadillo?
No? Well we got one in our basement,
Will you help me catch him?
Good—I'm gonna need your pillow.

Snatch that pillow and run out of the room yelling "we don't wanna kill 'em. We just wanna stun 'em!"

It's time to get up!
I love you, really I do.
But when it's Halloween,
I'm required to say BOO!

Optional accessory: Flashlight.
Not only is it required to say BOO on Halloween, dads are also encouraged to hold a flashlight below the chin, frighteningly illuminating the face while saying something scary in a Transylvanian accent—Ah, ah, ah!

It's time to get up!
And I've got some nasal congestion.
But anyway,
I've got a question.
Whaddya think of my duck impression?

(do your best nasally Quack)

As with most animal impressions, get real close and start in soft and expressive. Then raise the volume and cadence.

It's time to get up!
It's time to start reading.
If you do this with your wrist,
You can feel your heart beating.

(Two fingers on wrist)

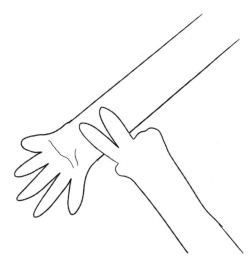

This one serves double duty. Not only will it help your child wake up, but it passes off a cub scout/girl scout award requirement. I checked.

It's time to get up!
I've got to get to a meeting
With the Japanese prime minister.
I need to practice my greeting:
O wa yo gozaimasu!

Feel free to meet with the prime minister of any other country—it doesn't really matter. However, they probably don't speak Japanese.

It's time to get up!
It's not time to doze.
Pardon me in advance
As I blow my nose.

After noisily filling up a tissue, employ your sleight of hand and place a damp paper towel on your child's forehead. They'll think it's hilarious!

It's time to get up!
You don't wanna be a flunky.
Would it help you get up
If I act like a monkey?

Alternate between high pitched screeches and low grunts, and chest beating. Try walking on your knuckles and liberally sniff in the general vicinity of your child's face.

It's time to get up!
It's not time to be cross.
What does cross mean, you ask?
Well, it's what they say in England
When you act like my boss.

Hopefully, your kids don't know your boss, and/or hopefully they don't misassociate your boss with your lovely wife.

"It's time to get up", said the prince to his horse.
The beast just sighed, and replied, "of course".
The prince grabbed his saddle and stopped with a shock.
He turned to his steed. "Did you just talk?"

Um, it's kind of urgent.
It's time to get up!
The police are outside—
"Come out with your hands up!"

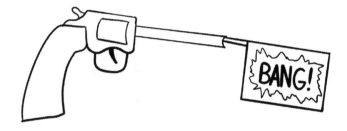

Peer out between the blinds with a worried look and a quavering voice.

It's time to get up!
Argh! What was I thinking?
Let me start over again,
This time without blinking.

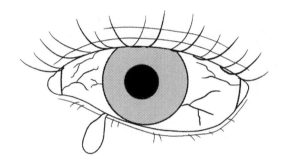

Get up close and STARE! Throw down the gauntlet and challenge your child to a staring contest.

It's time to get up!
It's not time to sleep in!
What's that honey? It's Saturday?
Oops, sorry! Did it again!

If your kids are like mine, they get a real kick out of good ol' dad making silly mistakes, like forgetting it's the weekend and waking everybody up two hours early.

It's time to get up!
At least your mom says it is.
If you don't get your butt out of bed,
You'll be in deep shiz!

This one's rated PG, and like any movie with mature language, your kids will be very tempted to start repeating it. Best to check with Mom before doing this one.

It's time to get up!
Today—an extra chore.
Please judge my impression
Of a wild boar.

Squeal ever so loudly.

It's time to get up!
Ooh, you're getting so big!
I think you're old enough
To learn an Irish jig.

Riverdance like there's no tomorrow. The main components are holding your hands behind your back, staring straight ahead with a serious expression, hopping on one foot, and using your other foot to alternate between kicking your knee and buttocks as fast as you possibly can.

It's time to get up!
It's not time to be funny.
And when I'm serious,
I act like a bunny.

Buck teeth and tiny noises. Maybe gnaw on a carrot while invading your child's personal space.

It's time to get up!
It's not time to dilly.
When I make this face,
Do you think I look silly?

Do the best you can.

It's time to get up!
Hey, you're getting taller!
Check out my moves.
I'm a pretty good baller.

Try spinning a basketball on your finger, and then try rolling it down
your arm and across your shoulders (emphasis on "try").

It's time to get up!
And I don't mean to boast.
In the kitchen mom's making
Her famous French toast!

If you remember, kindly ask your wife to not make a liar out of you.

It's time to get up!
It's hard, isn't it hun?
That's why I'm packing today
My little squirt gun!

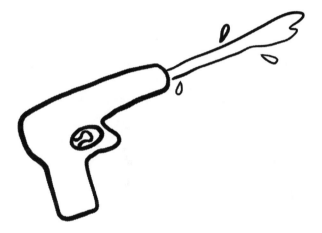

One squirt ought to do it.

It's time to get up!
The clock's a tickin'.
To get things moving,
Ima cluck like a chicken!

Take a little time to study how chickens move about the yard. There's more to it than you might realize. Not only do they cluck, they also crow, scratch in the dirt, eat anything nasty, and incessantly peck at smaller chickens.

It's time to get up!
It's seven o'clock.
Hey, put your tongue on this battery.
It doesn't really shock.

Best not to exceed the recommended 9-volt limit, and I dare you not
to try it yourself.

It's time to get up!
It's 7:01.
How would you feel
If I put my hair in a bun.

It might be worth investing in a wig.

It's time to get up!
It's 7:02.
Which one smells worse?
My left or right shoe?

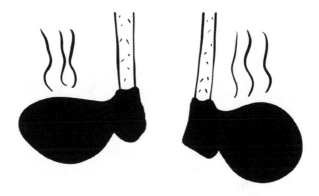

If you choose to use real shoes, consider using your child's own shoes. Then, when they get angry, you'll be able to smile and say, "but these are *your* shoes."

It's time to get up!
It's 7:03.
You've been sleeping so long,
I'm sure you have to pee.

Optional accessory: Two pitchers of water

Simulate a tiny waterfall by pouring water slowly from one pitcher to the other. The added realism will have your child heading toward the toilet in no time.

It's time to get up!
The alarm just went off.
Looks like I still have a cold
And this awful cough!

(hock up a lung)

It's time to get up!
Hey, something's out of place.
I know what it is.
It's that frown on your face.

(tickle time)

It's time to get up!
Stop sleeping, please.
Unless you're dreaming of nacho cheese.
If so, do continue, by all means.

Try out your best Barry White and then slowly chomp away at some tortilla chips. Leave the cheese in the fridge—we're going for maximum crunch. It works best if you try to chomp without completely closing your mouth. I've done some research on this.

It's time to get up!
Let's learn how to share.
You can share shirts and toys,
But not your underwear!

Consider gently placing a clean pair of underwear on the face of your child.

It's time to get up!
The alarm didn't work!
I'm sorry, but now
I have to be a jerk.

Flip the light on rapidly 10-15 times. Or softly flick an ear 10-15 times.

It's time to get up!
Wanna get to school early?
We'd better get started
Making your hair curly.

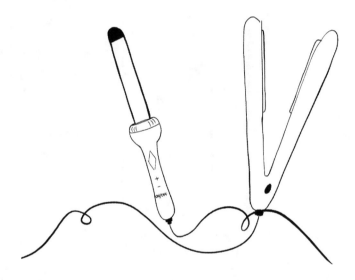

Come prepared with a curling iron or even a straightener for maximum clickiness.

It's time to get up!
Dingitty ding dong dings!
I heard you won't get out of bed,
Until the fat lady sings!

Traverse those octaves like a mountain goat through the Alps!

It's time to get up!
"Dad, stop it!"
But I need a friend.
Who wants to play Bop It?

Twist it, Pull it...I remember my first time playing Bop It. You're out!
(of bed)

It's time to get up,
Mr. Rip Van Winkle!
When you go to the bathroom,
Don't forget to tinkle.

Sometimes they forget.

It's time to get up!
Don't you gimme no sass!
I've got enough to worry about;
I chipped my tooth on this glass!

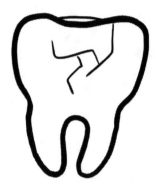

The Ol' Ring on the Glass Trick

Come into the bedroom holding a glass. After delivering the poem, make a show of taking a drink and just as the cup nears your lips, tap the glass with your ring finger. As soon as you hear the clink, react as if you just knocked out your front tooth. You'll probably want to practice this one a few times, and be careful. It's easy to hit your actual tooth!

It's time to get up!
Well, you're as happy as a lark!
I would be too,
If I didn't run into things in the dark.

Pretend to run into the door on your way out of the room.

It's time to get up!
Take a good long look—
It's the last time you'll see
Your precious little book!

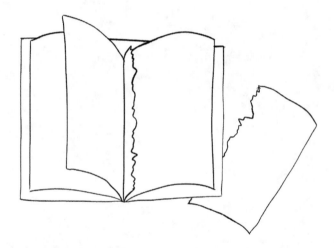

Most kids get a lot of satisfaction from destroying things. So, feed their natural inclinations and grab your child's favorite book. Hold it open in front of your mouth, and in a swift motion, pretend to tear a page from it while making a Ffffffffffft! noise. It's surprisingly satisfying and realistic!

It's time to get up,
My sweet little girl.
Did you know I like nuts
As much as a squirrel?

Crack actual nuts loudly and/or do your best impression of the animal, teeth and fingers.

It's time to get up!
Looks like it's gonna blizzard.
And just in the nick of time!
I've perfected my lizard!

(in the face, blank expression, tongue in and out quickly)

It's time to get up!
It's 7:33.
You know I'd let you sleep,
If it were up to me.
But it's not, you see.
Who? You asking me?
Sorry, I'm sworn to secrecy.

It's time to get up!
Could you please—actually no.
You're too tired.
I'll find someone else to play in the snow.

Save this one for the first Saturday morning snowfall.

It's time to get up!
It's 7:34.
It's the perfect morning,
To strengthen my core.

Start doing loud sit-ups next to the bed.

It's time to get up!
It's 7:35.
Do you hear that under your bed?
Sounds like a beehive!

See if you can set the record for the longest buzz without taking a breath.

It's time to get up!
It's 7:36.
Think I can finish this sucker
In 100 licks?

Slurp as loudly as you possibly can.

It's time to get up!
It's 7:37.
Just wanted you to know
We're changing your name to Kevin.

(or "we've decided to stick with the name Kevin")

It's time to get up!
It's 7:38.
You'll be happy to know,
We've set you up on a date.
Pretty sure they're your soulmate!

Show a picture of somebody not-so-scrumptious.

It's time to get up!
It's 7:39.
Is that a zit on your nose?
You can barely see it—you'll be fine!

Take your phone off silent mode and snap a picture. Then walk out of the room saying, "Honey! You've gotta see this!"

It's time to get up!
It's the first day of school.
Let's focus a little more this year
On being really cool.

Or less. Whatevs.

It's time to get up!
It's the last day of school.
Do you think you met your goal
Of being super cool?

It's time to get up!
It's Independence Day!
Since we're all Democrats
Let's hear that donkey bray!

Try as you might, it's impossible to make this sound beautiful. By the way, even if you're a faithful Republican, claiming that the family has switched allegiances will cause enough cognitive dissonance in your child's mind that he or she won't be able to sleep any longer.

It's time to get up!
I have no words.
I literally used this stone
To kill two birds.

Put a cold stone from the freezer in their hand—careful there's blood
on it.

It's time to get up!
It's 7:35.
Let me check that pulse.
Yep, you're still alive!

Best to be sure, so after checking your child's wrist, check the neck, and then use the tried and true method of foot-to-ear.

It's time to get up,
My little taquito!
If you be a good little niño (niña),
I'll getcha a breakfast burrito.

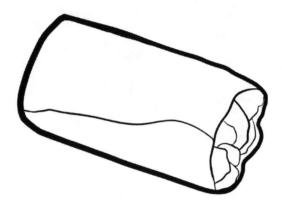

Do your best Mexican accent. For inspiration, watch Nacho Libre the night before.

It's time to get up!
You know how your mom's a total beauty?
That must be why
You're such a cutie!

Best to deliver this one while your wife is in earshot.

It's time to get up!
It's not time to play dumb.
Check out my new alarm clock sound—
Chomping gum!

Make a joyful noise! And don't forget to set the record for the biggest bubble blown before 7 a.m.

It's time to get up!
It's a beautiful day!
I'd like to take this moment,
To horse like a neigh.

Neigh enthusiastically, followed by loudly blowing air out of your mouth such that your cheeks and lips just a-quiver.

It's time to get up!
It's not time to cry.
I can't lie.
I'd probably cry, maybe even die,
If somebody poked me in the eye!

Grab your child's finger and poke your own eye. Start to cry.

It's time to get up!
Did you know I'm a robot too?
Let me demonstrate
By speaking binary to you.
(Beep. Beep. Beep. Bebop. Beep)

My machine learning algorithm predicts that it is best to deliver this entire poem in a monotone, robotic voice.

It's time to get up!
Just like fish in a barrel.
What's that you ask?
Just words to my new Christmas Carol

(sing loudly to the tune O Tannenbaum)

OH fish in a barrel!
OH fish in a barrel!
It's just like shooting fish in a barrel!
I sang my carol
To my best friend Daryl.
He agreed it's just like fish in a barrel.
OH fish in a barrel!
OH fish in a barrel!
It's just like shooting fish in a barrel!

It's time to get up!
I know what you lack.
You need a mighty vigorous
Rub on the back!

Pretend you're lighting a fire in the Yukon. You'll need a lot of friction!

It's time to get up!
Said Hermione with a bang.
Did you hear that Harry
Just kissed Cho Chang?

Harry fans will like this one. Hairy fans won't know what you're talking about.

It's time to get up!
But don't look over here!
I'm walking around
In my underweer!

Or depending on your humor tolerance and the situational need for shock value: "I'm trying on your underweer!"

It's time to get up!
And you gotta hustle!
If you need some inspiration,
Check out this new muscle.

Flex your bicep Arnold style—in fact, try delivering this poem in a barky Austrian accent. Then proceed to flex every other muscle in your body, grunting and bearing down loudly to encourage the audience to ooh and ahh.

It's time to get up!
It's time to go eat.
Looks like you're movin' slow today.
Yo! Drop the beat!
(beatbox: bomb, chi-bomb, bomb, bum CHAdda (chadda is octaves higher)
(repeat, replacing CHAdda with a child's name)

It's time to get up!
He's just not funny anymore.
You know that pig from the lion king?
He's such a boar!

Tweens (even groggy ones) are just starting to appreciate puns, so take advantage of it.

'Tis the night before Christmas!
So let's draw straws.
If you get the short one,
You get to meet Santa Claus!

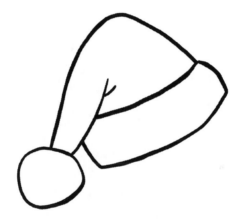

Bury the short straw in the palm of your hand. Let your kids pull all the long straws. Then show them that you're the one holding the short straw. FOILED AGAIN!

It's time to get up!
It's 65 degrees.
I need some assistance.
Will you help me find my keys?

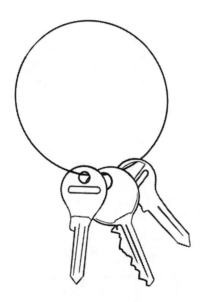

Reach under the pillow and pull out your car keys. Enthusiastically jiggle them near the child's ear, thanking them profusely for saving the day!

It's time to get up!
I may look like a fat man... (look around, make sure no one's looking)
But I'll tell you a secret.
I'm actually Batman.

They were going to find out eventually.

It's time to get up!
Oh, you've got a fever!
Let me cut this Tylenol in half,
With my meat cleaver.

Instructions:
1. Place Tylenol on a cutting board.
2. Strike the cutting board swiftly and loudly with a meat cleaver.
3. Retrieve the Tylenol pieces from the floor.
4. Put the pieces back in the bottle.
5. Do not try this at home.

It's time to get up!
Too bad we're not in Disneyland.
'Cause I'm Mickey Mouse!
And I'd shake your hand! Ha ha!

Awaken the counter-tenor in you, and don't forget to get the laugh right at the end. It's quick and the second "ha" shoots into the stratosphere.

It's time to get up!
Don't be afraid.
Just got some scissors.
Gonna trim your braid.

You don't even need to bring scissors to this party. Just touching the braid should be enough to get your little girl up. In fact, your child might instinctively bat away your hand, and you don't want to be holding a sharp implement at that moment.

It's time to get up!
Wait, what did you say?
Oh, I thought you were already up.
That'll be the day!

If your house is a "sarcasm free zone", then move on people. Nothing to see here.

It's time to get up!
Ever have deja vu?
It's time to get up!
Ever have deja vu?

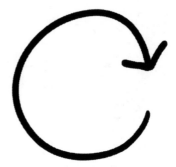

Rinse and repeat.

It's time to get up!
It's time for sunrise yoga!
I've decided to skip the spandex,
And pose in my toga.

Wrap yourself in a white sheet, greet your children with a hearty namaste and hit Warrior One hard.

It's time to get up!
Ooh, your bed looks too hot!
Let's try an experiment.
Blankets or not?

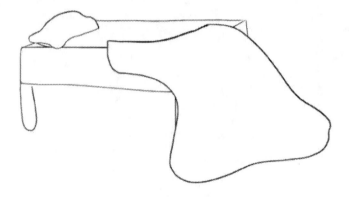

Imagine you're a magician yanking a tablecloth out from under a table full of precious china.

It's time to get up!
Sleeping in is your proclivity.
Let me share one of mine:
Testing feet sensitivity.

It's never too early for a vocabulary quiz.

It's time to get up!
Hey, you're not wearing any socks!
That means you're unprotected,
From my electric shocks!

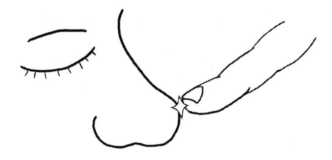

Don your wool socks and make a few trips up and down the hallway.
Your index finger is a surprisingly good conductor of electricity.

It's time to get up!
I know that you're sleepy.
But I need to talk to you.
I'm feeling rather weepy.

Immediately dive right into your impression of an emotionally unstable
tween. For example:

I'm sorry—
It's just that—
My kids won't get up.
They're always late for school.
And I'm always late for work.
And my clothes don't fit.
And I don't have any friends!

It's time to get up!
It's not time to play dead.
If you can't get up,
I'll have to shave your head.

Make a click noise then see how long you can keep a buzz sound going as you move whatever implement around your child's head.

It's time to get up!
It's not time to sleep.
What kind of car did you want?
Was it a Porsche or a Jeep?

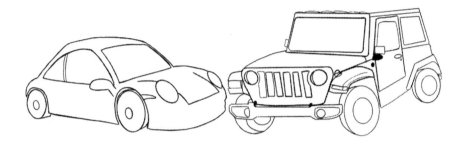

Better start saving that allowance...

Printed in the United States
by Baker & Taylor Publisher Services